Inaya

Written by Amara Sharif
Illustrated by Katia Kolesnik

Bear

Panda

Parrot

Snake

Elephant

Monkey

Lion

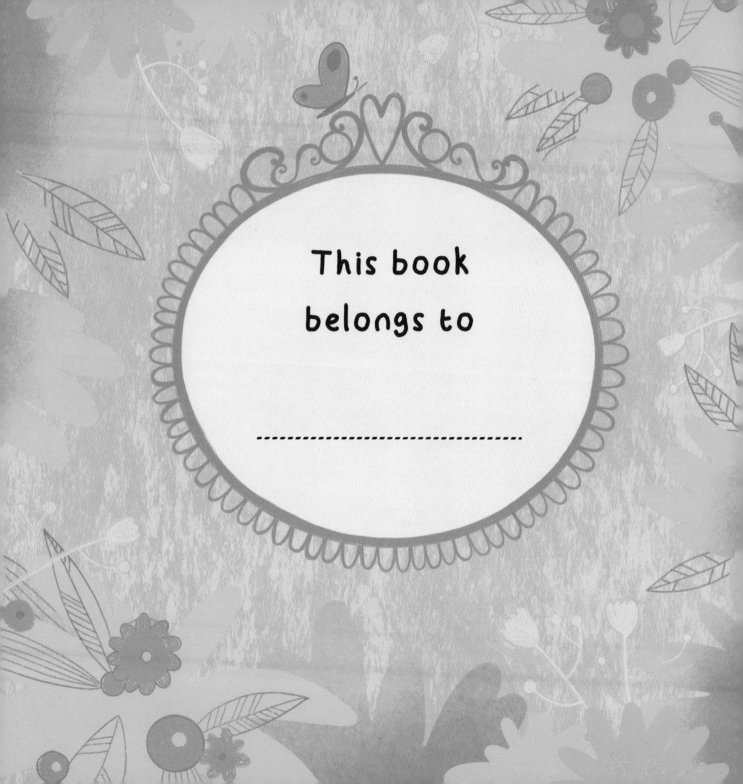

This book
belongs to

Inaya and her best friend Nia went to the Zoo.

Oo! Oo! Oo! Shouted the monkey swinging from the tree.

Roar! Replied the lion licking his furry mane.

Squawk! Sang the parrot spreading out her colourful wings.

Hiss! Whispered the snake slithering into a ball.

Pawoo! Trumpeted the elephant splashing water everywhere.

PANDA

Growl! Yawned the bear as she settled down to sleep.

Help Inaya and Nia find a path to the animals

Draw a line to the food that each animal eats

For my adventurers Inaya Noor and Nauman
- Amara

FIRST EDITION

Dear Qundeel,

Thank you for allowing me the opportunity to showcase my book. May Allah bless you.

Amara

x

Printed in Poland
by Amazon Fulfillment
Poland Sp. z o.o., Wrocław

85434569R00016